This journal belongs to

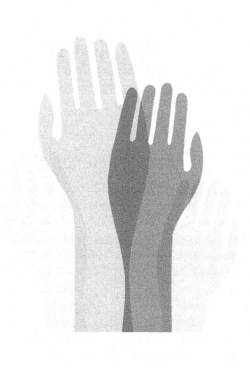

Light For Your Purpose Journey

Igniting Your Passion to Discover, Embrace, and Fulfill Your Kingdom Calling

Gilles Gentley

LIGHT FOR YOUR PURPOSE JOURNEY
Igniting Your Passion to Discover, Embrace, and Fulfill Your Kingdom Calling

Published by ILLUMINATION PRESS

ATLANTA, GA

Copyright ©2023 by Gilles Gentley. All rights reserved.

No part of this book may be reproduced in any form or by any mechanical means, including information storage and retrieval systems, without permission in writing from the publisher/author, except by a reviewer who may quote passages in a review.

All images, logos, quotes, and trademarks included in this book are subject to use according to trademark and copyright laws of the United States of America.

ISBN:

Cover and Interior design by August Pride, LLC
All rights reserved by Gilles Gentley.
Printed in the United States of America.

ILLUMINATION PRESS
c/o Benecia Ponder
1100 Peachtree Street
Suite 250
Atlanta, GA 30309

Inspire@InspirationalAuthors.com
www.InspirationalAuthors.com

A Journey to Find Your Purpose

I am sure you are like me and have looked up at the sky, seen the vastness of the stars, and wondered why you are here.

I know every person has wrestled with this question in their life. Some of history's most remarkable men and women have had to ask and answer this question, and usually, that is why we know their names today.

I am passionate about living purposefully because I spent so many years living without direction or focus. I believed the lie that I was a mistake, and because of that, I lived as a mistake.

Isn't it great how in football, when the defense messes up, the offense gets a free play? That's when the game gets thrilling, and the quarterback can take daring risks, attempting passes they wouldn't otherwise have tried.

That's the approach I used early in my life.

Since I thought I was a mistake, I took chances and did things that others might not. Ultimately, this mindset led me to a life of addiction, deeply hurting the people I loved.

It wasn't until I opened the Bible that I discovered I was not a mistake—God put me here for a purpose.

...

Not that I have already obtained all this or have already arrived at my goal, but I press on to take hold of that for which Christ Jesus took hold of me.

Brothers and sisters, I do not consider myself yet to have taken hold of it. But one thing I do: Forgetting what is behind and straining toward what is ahead, I press on toward the goal to win the prize for which God has called me heavenward in Christ Jesus.

Philippians 3:12-14
...

Are you feeling stuck in the rut of life and not sure why you're here?

As you can tell from the condensed version 9f my story, I've been there too, which is why I'm so passionate about this subject.

I believe that God has a purpose for each of us, and it's up to us to embrace it.

If you look at Paul, he understood that God had called him for a purpose, and he spent all his days trying to fulfill that call.

In Ephesians 2:10, we're reminded that God created us with foreknowledge of our lives and that He's given us specific tasks to accomplish. Just think, out of billions of people in the world. God chose you and has good works only for you. Incredible thought, right?

The starting point is to believe that God has chosen you and that He has a life of purpose for you. If you don't believe in the Bible or the God of the Bible, this book might not be for you. But if you do, I have something special in store for you.

We'll take the next 21 days to go on a journey of purposeful living.

Let's do this!

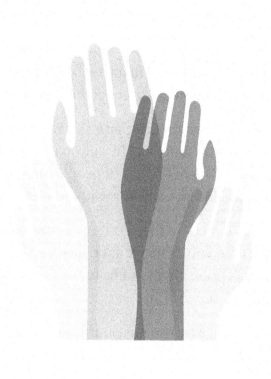

DAY 1

Stating Your Purpose

The Apostle Paul had a purpose statement. In 1 Corinthians 2:2, he said, "For I decided to know nothing among you except Jesus Christ and him crucified."

If you know the New Testament, then you know Paul and that his life was spent preaching and teaching Jesus. He was not concerned about his comfort or convenience. He did not strive to make himself known. His Focus was entirely on his purpose.

There's nothing more important than having a clear sense of purpose. It's the key to unlocking your true potential and guiding all of your decisions.

It's a powerful tool you can use to filter out distractions and align your actions with your deepest convictions. Whether you're facing a tough decision or seeking meaning in your everyday life, your purpose statement will be your North Star, pointing you towards the path God has for you.

Use the space below to write your purpose statement.

Now write a prayer asking God to help you live out your purpose and find ways to live on purpose.

_____
_____
_____
_____
_____
_____
_____
_____
_____
_____
_____
_____
_____
_____
_____
_____
_____
_____
_____
_____

DAY 2

Align Your Plans with God's Purpose

I've heard that a goal without a plan is just a dream. You are not a dreamer; you are a doer.

> The Bible says it this way— Many are the plans in a person's heart, but it is the LORD's purpose that prevails.
>
> **Proverbs 19:21**

It's important to remember that even though we have plans, God gets the final say. Having a plan is good, but it is better to have God's purpose.

Write out what you've planned for the next few years. What would you like to do or accomplish? Your plans could include finishing your degree, opening a business, or having a family.

_____
_____
_____
_____
_____
_____
_____
_____
_____
_____
_____
_____
_____
_____
_____
_____
_____
_____
_____
_____
_____
_____

Now, examine your plans using the filter of your purpose. Will these plans help you fulfill your purpose statement?

_____
_____
_____
_____
_____
_____
_____
_____
_____
_____
_____
_____
_____
_____
_____
_____
_____
_____
_____

Now that your plans are written down let's ask God to bless them.

Dear God,

I come to You with a heart full of gratitude and humility, seeking Your divine guidance and help as I pursue my goals in life. I know You have a unique purpose for me, and I ask that You help me align my goals with Your purpose.

Lord, I pray that You give me clarity of mind and wisdom to discern the goals aligned with Your will and purpose for my life. Help me to prioritize these goals above all others and to stay focused on them, even in the face of distractions and obstacles.

Father, I ask that You provide me with the resources and support I need to achieve my goals. Whether it's financial, emotional, or physical support, I trust You will provide for me according to Your abundant grace and love.

Most importantly, Lord, I pray that my goals will bring glory to Your name and serve Your kingdom's purposes. Help me to use the gifts and talents You have given me to make a positive impact on the world around me and to be a witness of Your love and grace.

Thank You, God, for Your unending faithfulness and willingness to guide me along the path You have set for me. May my goals align with Your will, and may I fulfill the purpose You have created for me.

In Jesus' Name, I pray. Amen.

DAY 3

Count Your Blessings

Having the right mindset is crucial in understanding and living our purpose. For the next few days, we will focus on an abundance mindset.

Steven Covey made this mindset famous in his 1989 book, Seven Habits of Highly Effective People.

I would argue that God told us about this mindset in the Bible. Let us talk about this and see if you agree with me.

Today, I want to talk about counting our blessings. It may sound contradictory to have an abundance mindset yet being happy with what we have, but the Bible says this is a secret of happiness.

Take a look at what the Bible says in 1 Thessalonians 5:16-18–

Rejoice always, pray without ceasing, and give thanks in all circumstances; for this is the will of God in Christ Jesus for you.

We see right here what God's will is for us—to be thankful for everything.

One of my favorite verses is Psalm 103:2

Bless the LORD, O my soul,
and forget not all his benefits.
We are commanded to give thanks
and not forget God's blessings.

Take a minute to reflect on what you have right now. Write out a list of what you are thankful to have in your life.

_____
_____
_____
_____
_____
_____
_____
_____
_____
_____
_____
_____
_____
_____
_____
_____
_____
_____
_____
_____
_____
_____
_____

Write out a prayer thanking God for what you have.

DAY 4

Developing A Can Do Mindset

Henry Ford made a profound statement when he said, "Whether you think you can or you think you can't – you're right."

This goes back to our abundance mindset. You are reading this book because you want to discover and follow your purpose. Developing a strong mindset is critical to accomplishing that mission.

While in jail awaiting trial, the Apostle Paul said, "I can do all things through Christ who strengthens me." (Philippians 4:13)

His mindset allowed him to endure all he went through.

I am not sure what you are going through, but I am confident you can get through them and achieve God's plan.

Get rid of those limiting mindsets, and find a bright outlook to make better choices.

Think of what negative beliefs you have about yourself or your situation. Now I want you to write down those thoughts but make them positive.

Examples:

I can do that thing, and I deserve to write a book.

I am smart enough, good enough, and worthy to lay hold of that.

_____

_____

_____

_____

_____

_____

_____

_____

_____

_____

_____

_____

_____

_____

_____

_____

_____

_____

Dear Heavenly Father,

I come before You with a heart full of gratitude and thanksgiving. I am so grateful for the gift of life that You have given me and for the countless blessings that You have bestowed upon me.

Today, I am particularly thankful for the promise that I can do everything through You, as stated in Philippians 4:13.

Father, I am humbled by the knowledge that I am nothing without Your strength and guidance. But with You by my side, I can achieve great things. Thank You for the power and grace You have bestowed upon me, enabling me to face each day with courage and confidence.

Lord, I ask that You continue to empower me through Your Holy Spirit so that I may always have the strength to do Your will and fulfill Your purposes for my life. Help me remain steadfast in my faith, even amid trials and difficulties, knowing that Your grace is sufficient for me.

Thank You, Lord, for Your never-ending love and faithfulness. May Your Name be glorified in all I do, and may my life be a testament to Your goodness and grace. In Jesus' Name, I pray. Amen.

DAY 5

Take Responsibility

To lay hold of your purpose, you must take responsibility for your life. Taking responsibility means realizing that every circumstance in your life results from your decisions. Not anyone else's.

Sometimes, certain situations are beyond your control, but your decisions and responses are still your responsibility. When we take responsibility for finding our purpose, fulfillment will follow.

Maybe you had unfair things happen to you as a child. Perhaps a spouse did things that impacted you negatively.

I am not saying that you are responsible for their actions; I am saying that as a person on a quest to lay hold of your purpose, you have a choice to make. You can keep playing the victim, or you can triumph despite your challenges.

I encourage you to tell the unfair thing that happened to you—I will work on forgiveness and healing and strive to lay hold of the things Jesus laid hold of me.

James 4:17 says, "So whoever knows the right thing to do and fails to do it, for him it is a sin."

My question to you is, What things in your life right now can you control? What areas of your life can you take responsibility for and choose to make right or better? Ask God to show you and list the things for which you can take responsibility.

_____

_____

_____

_____

_____

_____

_____

_____

_____

_____

_____

_____

_____

_____

_____

_____

_____

_____

_____

_____

_____

_____

Now take a few minutes to ask God to help you to take responsibility for these areas of your life. Write out a prayer asking God to help you. You can not do this alone; you will need God's help.

_____
_____
_____
_____
_____
_____
_____
_____
_____
_____
_____
_____
_____
_____
_____
_____
_____
_____
_____
_____
_____
_____

_____
_____
_____
_____
_____
_____
_____
_____
_____
_____
_____
_____
_____
_____
_____
_____
_____
_____
_____
_____

I know that you can do this with His help and your will. I believe in you.

DAY 6

What Do You Need?

What things do you need to fulfill your purpose?

If you are trying to lose weight and get in shape, you need food and exercise equipment.

If you want to start a business or become a life coach, you need clients.

There is always a needs list to help us achieve all we think we want. To fulfill your purpose, you probably don't need a shiny new peloton or that client list. As Maslow put it, there is a basic hierarchy of human needs. We need food and shelter, safety and people who care about us, healthy self-esteem, and self-actualization.

I would argue that we need a personal connection with our Creator more critically than any of these. God has made you for a particular purpose and without a relationship with our Creator, how can we know our purpose?

Tony Robbins has also given us a list of six human needs that sound a little like Maslow's.

I agree with what Maslow says about this, but I still maintain that most of his list can be met with a relationship with Jesus Christ. As you grow in your relationship with Jesus, He will show you what areas you need, and He can help provide them for you.

How can you need significance when the God of the universe has a particular assignment just for you?

How can you need certainty when you know the One that has made the moon and stars?

As we grow as humans and Christians, Jesus points out the things in our life that are not of Him. So, I ask you, what things in your life right now are things you need to help you fulfill your purpose in Jesus? Pray about this and ask God to show you the areas you need to achieve your goal. Write out a list of what God is leading you to do.

_____

_____

_____

_____

_____

_____

_____

_____

_____

_____

Dear Jesus,

I come to You today with a heart full of gratitude and thanksgiving. Thank You for meeting all of our needs, both big and small. Your love for us is overwhelming, and Your provision is abundant.

Thank You for Your faithfulness and always being there for us, even when we don't deserve it. Thank You for the ways You provide for us, whether through the people in our lives, the opportunities that come our way, or the blessings we receive.

Thank You for the ways that You comfort us in times of sorrow and for the ways that You guide us through difficult situations. You are our rock and refuge; we can always depend on You.

Thank You for Your grace and Your mercy and for the ways that You have provided salvation for us through Your death and resurrection. May we never take for granted the incredible gift You have given us.

Lord, please continue to meet our needs and guide us on the path You have set. Help us trust in You completely, knowing You will never disappoint us.

In Your Name, we pray, Amen.

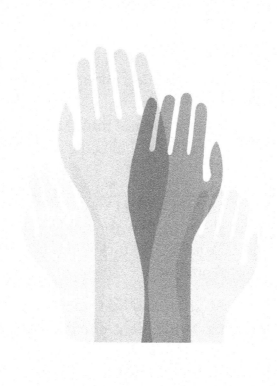

DAY 7

Battling The Inner Enemy

We are a week into this study, and I wonder if you heard a voice telling you that you can't do it.

I want to believe that you are not, but we all struggle with limiting beliefs. We have used this scripture, which is pertinent to our discussion today. Philippians 4:13 Paul says, "I can do all things through Jesus who strengthens me." This verse is not about throwing a football or some other way; contemporary Christianity has taken it out of context. Paul says that whatever situation we find ourselves in, God can help us get through it. It also means that whatever God has called you to do, He will help get you through that.

Our Limiting beliefs are like Goliath, which comes out and taunts us, telling us that we can't do it or that God cannot use us. If we allow that giant to come out and say things, we will always stay on the sidelines and be intimidated. We cannot move forward unless we believe that God can do something through us and He will provide strength. Today we are going to confront that giant and learn to silence him.

Write down your limiting beliefs below, and expose them thoughts.

_____
_____
_____
_____
_____
_____
_____
_____
_____
_____
_____
_____
_____
_____
_____
_____
_____
_____
_____
_____
_____
_____
_____

Now rewrite your thoughts to make them positive and include God in them. Instead of thinking there is no way I can write a book, say with God's help, I am smart enough, and I can write a book. I can get that promotion, and God is going to help me. I can be the best mother to my son. Your turn, write them down and believe them.

_____
_____
_____
_____
_____
_____
_____
_____
_____
_____
_____
_____
_____
_____
_____
_____
_____
_____

Now write down a prayer thanking God that you can do it. Write with faith and believe that God can and will help you.

___

DAY 8

What Trips Your Trigger?

What things do you do that you love to do? What are you good at?

Are you good at art and wish you could spend your days doing art? When the boss asks who wants to make a presentation, does that excite you? When you see people's reactions to your presentation, does that fill you with joy?

It seems basic to say, but what gives you joy, more than likely, is your purpose.

Write down a list of things that make you happy and the things you are good at. It's a short list; this is not a shot at you, but it won't be long if it's your purpose.

_____
_____
_____
_____
_____
_____
_____
_____
_____
_____
_____
_____
_____
_____
_____
_____
_____
_____

Colossians 3:23 says,

"Whatever you do, work at it with all your heart, as working for the Lord, not for human masters,"

As you do your hobby, ask God to help you find ways to serve Jesus and make money with your passion. I believe that it is key that you want to be able to serve Jesus and support yourself. We might not be talking about a career change, but we are talking about a mind shift and an attitude change.

Write a prayer to God asking Him to show you how to utilize your passion for serving Him and making money.

___

DAY 9

Bring Your Purpose To Life

The Japanese term Ikigai (pronounced ee-key-guy) merges the words iki, which signifies "alive" or "life" and gai, which refers to "benefit" or "worth."

The amalgamation of these terms conveys what makes one's life meaningful, valuable, or purposeful. It resembles the French phrase raison d'etre or "reason for being."

The concept of Ikigai is deeply ingrained in Japanese culture and is seen as a fundamental part of leading a fulfilling life. In Japan, it is common for individuals to spend their entire lives searching for their Ikigai, and it is considered an ongoing process rather than a single destination.

Ikigai is believed to arise from the intersection of four elements: what you love, what you are good at, what the world needs, and what you can be paid for.

By balancing these elements, individuals can discover their Ikigai and live a life of purpose and satisfaction. The concept of Ikigai has gained popularity beyond Japan and has become a source of inspiration for individuals seeking to find meaning and fulfillment in their lives.

In Philippians 3:13, the Apostle Paul said that he presses on to lay hold of that which Christ laid hold of him.

Ikigai is more self-serving than what we are talking about in this section. God has chosen you for a purpose and given you gifts and talents that are specific to you. He chose this because He wants you to help spread the gospel. Let's find your ikigai or reason for being.

What things do you love?

What are you good at?

What does the world need?

The world needs Jesus. What can you do to introduce Jesus to those around you.?

___

The last part is what you can get paid for. So look at your list and ask yourself, what can I get paid for that I love and the world needs?

___

DAY 10

Be Honest With Yourself

To discover your purpose, it's essential to acknowledge your limitations and avoid getting frustrated with yourself.

Take the time to understand yourself, gradually assuming the role of an observer. By practicing self-compassion and building self-awareness, you can uncover the meaning you seek.

When feeling lost in life, practicing self-compassion means being patient with yourself. While it can be disorienting not to know your purpose, remember that uncertainty is a natural starting point for everyone who has ever asked themselves this question.

Embrace your hesitancy and use it as a catalyst to delve deeper and uncover a greater sense of meaning.

• • •

> "Come to me, all you who are weary and burdened, and I will give you rest. Take my yoke upon you and learn from me, for I am gentle and humble in heart, and you will find rest for your souls. For my yoke is easy and my burden is light."

Matthew 11:28-30 NIV

• • •

It is easy to get overwhelmed by the things we are not good at. As you reflect on what you are passionate about and what you are good at, you will find things you are not as gifted at.

Maybe you are passionate about something but not good at it. It will take work. I remember wanting to preach the word of God, but I was not a great speaker. I didn't even know how to write a sermon. I had to work on both things and I often felt overwhelmed and frustrated. What I did not do was let my frustration get me to a point where I threw in the towel and gave up on what God called me to do.

Give yourself some grace. It is ok to not be good at everything and to struggle in some areas of your life.

Write God a letter asking Him to help you have grace with yourself and to show you how to grow in areas you struggle in.

_____
_____
_____
_____
_____
_____
_____
_____
_____
_____
_____
_____
_____
_____
_____
_____
_____
_____
_____
_____
_____

DAY 11

Be Grateful

According to the Word of God, gratitude is a powerful emotion that can lead to abundance. The Bible encourages us to give thanks in all circumstances, as this is God's will for us in Christ Jesus. Furthermore, the benefits of practicing gratitude are well-documented in scientific research, such as improved mental health, stronger relationships, and enhanced personal happiness.

One of the simplest ways to cultivate a grateful heart is by keeping a gratitude journal. In the Book of Psalms, we are urged to give thanks to the Lord and praise His name. Writing down things we are thankful for each day can help us to do just that. As we reflect on our blessings and express gratitude, we can experience a shift in our perspective and outlook on life.

Gratitude meditation is another practice that can help us develop a habit of thankfulness. The Bible tells us to meditate on God's Word day and night. We can apply this same principle to focus on the good things in our lives. Through meditation, we can quiet our minds, be present in the moment, and cultivate an attitude of appreciation for all the blessings we have received. By practicing gratitude daily, we can honor God and live abundantly and joyfully.

Write out a list of things that you are grateful for in your life today!

Think about your spiritual journey as a Christian over the past year. What are three specific ways you have grown in your faith, and what events or experiences contributed to that growth? Offer thanks for these opportunities and ask for continued guidance in your walk with Christ.

_____
_____
_____
_____
_____
_____
_____
_____
_____
_____
_____
_____
_____
_____
_____
_____
_____
_____
_____

Sometimes, God works in mysterious ways, and blessings can come disguised as challenges or setbacks. Reflect on a difficult time in your life and identify at least one hidden blessing that emerged from that experience. How has this realization deepened your faith and trust in God's plan for your life?

_____
_____
_____
_____
_____
_____
_____
_____
_____
_____
_____
_____
_____
_____
_____
_____
_____

DAY 12

Get Grounded In The Word

As you begin your search for God's purpose, it's essential to remember that the primary way He speaks to us is through the Bible. Scripture can guide us on our journey and help us understand the heart of God. Therefore, it's crucial to start delving into the Word of God to gain clarity and direction.

In Psalm 119:105, we read, "Your word is a lamp to my feet and a light to my path."

This verse emphasizes the significance of God's Word in our lives. Scripture is a light that illuminates the path we need to take and helps us navigate through the darkness. As we read and meditate on the Bible, we can gain wisdom and understanding and find direction for our lives.

Studying the Bible teaches us how to live wisely in God's world. Proverbs 4:7 reminds us, "The beginning of wisdom is this: Get wisdom, and whatever you get, get insight."

We can take the first step toward discovering our purpose by gaining insight and understanding from the Word of God. As we immerse ourselves in Scripture and seek to understand God's heart, we can trust He will guide us toward His plan for our lives.

You won't find a scripture that tells you to become a painter, write a book, or do some things God calls you to. That doesn't mean God won't speak to you and call you to do those things.

What verses has God been using to speak into your life?

_____

_____

_____

_____

_____

_____

_____

_____

_____

_____

_____

_____

_____

_____

_____

_____

Write a prayer to God using your verses, asking God to show you your purpose

_____
_____
_____
_____
_____
_____
_____
_____
_____
_____
_____
_____
_____
_____
_____
_____
_____
_____
_____
_____
_____
_____
_____

DAY 13

Count The Costs

• • •

Large crowds were traveling with Jesus, and turning to them he said: "If anyone comes to me and does not hate father and mother, wife and children, brothers and sisters—yes, even their own life—such a person cannot be my disciple. And whoever does not carry their cross and follow me cannot be my disciple.

Luke 14:25-27 NIV

• • •

In this passage, Jesus teaches that following Him requires a deep commitment and sacrifice. He asks His followers to give up everything, including their relationships and lives, to serve and obey Him fully.

In the following verses, Luke 14:28-33, Jesus continues by illustrating the importance of counting the cost of discipleship. He compares it to building a tower or going to war, saying that anyone who doesn't take the time to consider the cost will fail carefully.

In the same way, anyone who wants to follow Jesus must be willing to pay the price, which may include facing persecution, rejection, and even death. However, Jesus also emphasizes that the reward of following Him is worth the cost, as it leads to eternal life.

Finally, Luke 14:34-35 concludes by warning that half-hearted commitment is not enough. Jesus says that if salt loses its saltiness, it is no longer helpful and should be thrown out. In the same way, anyone who claims to be a disciple of Jesus but does not fully commit themselves to Him will not be able to serve Him truly. This passage teaches that following Jesus requires wholehearted devotion and a willingness to pay whatever price is necessary. Still, it also promises that the reward of eternal life is well worth it.

Your purpose will cost you. I don't know what it is, but it will cost you. Leonard Ravenhill said, "You know one thing about a man carrying a cross outside the city: you know he isn't going to be coming back."

Are you prepared to pay the price for your calling? Take a minute and think about the price of fulfilling God's purpose for your life, and write out what you think it will cost.

_____
_____
_____
_____
_____
_____
_____
_____
_____
_____
_____
_____
_____
_____
_____
_____
_____
_____
_____
_____

As Jesus was in the garden, He prayed to the Father to remove the obligation of death on the cross, and then He said, "Not my will, but your will be done."

Take a minute and pray, committing to God that His will be done with your life no matter what the cost is.

_____

_____

_____

_____

_____

_____

_____

_____

_____

_____

_____

_____

_____

_____

_____

_____

_____

DAY 14

Your Purpose Is Not Your Own!

I know what you are thinking; we have spent a few weeks discussing my purpose, and you now tell me it's not mine.

Correct.

• • •

> For in him all things were created: things in heaven and on earth, visible and invisible, whether thrones or powers or rulers or authorities; all things have been created through him and for him.
>
> **Colossians 1:16 NIV**

• • •

God created you. The purpose that He has given you is for Him and His glory. The Westminster Shorter Catechism says that the chief end of man is to glorify God and enjoy Him forever. Your purpose is to glorify God and to enjoy Him.

Does your purpose line up with this?

Will the things you are doing bring glory to God? Maybe more critically, does it allow you to enjoy God?

Reflect on your daily activities and interactions with others. Identify two specific ways you can use your unique talents and abilities to serve others and glorify God in your everyday life. How can these acts of service help you enjoy a deeper connection with God and find joy in living out your faith?

Consider your hobbies, interests, and passions. How can you integrate your love for God into these activities and use them as a platform to glorify Him? Describe one instance where you have felt God's presence while engaging in your passion, and how it has enhanced your enjoyment and appreciation for His creation.

Take a moment now and write a prayer to God asking Him to help you do things that glorify Him and enjoy him.

_____
_____
_____
_____
_____
_____
_____
_____
_____
_____
_____
_____
_____
_____
_____
_____
_____
_____
_____
_____

DAY 15

Actively Seek God's Will

You may have noticed you have yet to live up to your real purpose during this time. After all, that is why you bought this book and have been working on yourself. Before this, you may have been thinking you are living your purpose but have been missing it.

Living in our God-given purpose is crucial for believers in Christ. Although God is sovereign and works all things according to His purposes, we can make choices that align with or deviate from His will. Psalm 57:2 reminds us that God fulfills His purpose for us, but we are also responsible for seeking and obeying His will.

In Ephesians 5:15-17, Paul urges believers to make the most of their time and understand the Lord's will. This means we must actively seek God's will and make choices that align with His purposes. Doing so, we can find greater fulfillment and purpose in our lives.

However, when we neglect to seek God's will and then make choices that deviate from His purposes, we may experience a sense of emptiness and aimlessness. Proverbs 14:12 warns, "There is a way that seems right to a man, but its end is the way to death."

It is important to remember that not all paths we take in life will lead to God's intended purpose for us. Therefore, we must remain vigilant in seeking God's will and making choices that align with His purposes.

Ask God to show you what things you have been pursuing that are not of Him. Write down what those things are.

_____
_____
_____
_____
_____
_____
_____
_____
_____
_____
_____
_____
_____
_____
_____
_____
_____

Now pray and ask God to help you not go back to those things and to make the most of the time you have left

___

___

___

___

___

___

___

___

___

___

___

___

___

___

___

___

___

___

___

___

DAY 16

Build A Strong Support System

• • •

Walk with the wise and become wise, for a companion of fools suffers harm.

Proverbs 13:20 NIV

• • •

Our relationships are essential, and who we hang out with is critical to reaching our purpose.

Who is the most important person in your life right now? Do they help you reach your goals or drag you down? Do you have a person that can add value to your life? What relationships do you need to maintain, and what ones do you need to eliminate?

I am not saying you can't be friends with people in your life, but if they don't help you reach your goals, you need to spend more time with people that help you.

During this time, have you thought about certain people doing what you want to do? Reach out to these people and see if you can meet with them. Think about what questions you would like to ask them.

Proverbs 13:20 states, "Walk with the wise and become wise, for a companion of fools suffers harm." Reflect on your current support system and the people you spend the most time with. How do these individuals influence your life positively or negatively? Identify two specific ways you can strengthen your circle by surrounding yourself with wise and supportive friends who will uplift and encourage you in your journey.

_____

_____

_____

_____

_____

_____

_____

_____

_____

_____

_____

_____

_____

_____

Think about someone in your life who embodies wisdom and good character, as described in Proverbs 13:20. Write about a situation where their guidance or example has had a positive impact on your life. How can you continue to learn from this person and incorporate their wisdom into your own actions and decisions? Consider ways to deepen your relationship with them and express gratitude for their presence in your life.

_____
_____
_____
_____
_____
_____
_____
_____
_____
_____
_____
_____
_____
_____
_____
_____
_____

Reflect on your own role as a friend and support to others in your circle. How can you be a positive influence and encourage those around you to make wise choices and live in accordance with their values? Identify one specific action or change you can make in your own behavior to be a better source of support and inspiration for your friends and loved ones. Consider the impact this change could have on your relationships and personal growth.

_____

_____

_____

_____

_____

_____

_____

_____

_____

_____

_____

_____

_____

_____

_____

DAY 17

Find Purpose In Pain

In his book, The Problem with Pain, C.S. Lewis said, "Pain insists on being heard. God shouts to us in our pain. It is His megaphone to rouse a deaf world."

For better or worse, pain is often our greatest teacher. It shows us how strong we are and what areas we can work on. I don't want us to dwell on the painful things in our life, but what have you gone through, and what lessons did you learn?

One of the worst things is to go through something and endure pain and not learn from it. So take a little time and consider the lessons you learned during your most painful times.

One caveat about this prompt: Do not spend TOO much time on this. It's not healthy to dwell on negative things for long.

Romans 8:28 says, "And we know that in all things God works for the good of those who love him, who have been called according to his purpose." Reflect on a painful or challenging experience you have faced. How can you find purpose in this situation by recognizing God's hand at work? Identify one positive outcome or lesson learned from this experience that has contributed to your personal growth or understanding of God's plan for your life.

_____
_____
_____
_____
_____
_____
_____
_____
_____
_____
_____
_____
_____
_____
_____
_____

Painful experiences can sometimes cause us to question our faith or God's intentions. Consider a time when you struggled to understand why something painful happened to you. How did you eventually come to trust God's plan and see the bigger picture? Write about the process of surrendering control and trusting in God's wisdom and love, even during difficult times.

_____
_____
_____
_____
_____
_____
_____
_____
_____
_____
_____
_____
_____
_____
_____
_____
_____
_____
_____

Our own experiences with pain can deepen our empathy and compassion for others who face similar challenges. Reflect on a time when your personal struggles allowed you to better understand and support someone else going through a difficult period. How did this shared experience help you both to find hope and comfort in God's promise, as described in Romans 8:28?.

_____

_____

_____

_____

_____

_____

_____

_____

_____

_____

_____

_____

_____

_____

_____

_____

DAY 18

Your Eternal Purpose

Paul was beaten and jailed. He was shipwrecked as well as stoned. Peter was crucified upside down.

John was banished to the Island of Patmos.

Nero set Christians on fire and used them for sport in the Coliseum.

I do not want you to be ignorant that the call of God is both a blessing and a curse. You will endure hardship for the cause of Christ. Know that whatever you face in this life is but for a fleeting moment.

• • •

Therefore we do not lose heart. Though outwardly we are wasting away, yet inwardly we are being renewed day by day. For our light and momentary troubles are achieving for us an eternal glory that far outweighs them all. So we fix our eyes not on what is seen, but on what is unseen, since what is seen is temporary, but what is unseen is eternal.

2 Corinthians 4:16-18 NIV

• • •

As much as what we are doing is for us here on Earth, you must remember that God is more concerned with your eternity. Your purpose in life is to get ready for your eternal life.

Write down how you feel when you think of this and what God is speaking to you about your eternal purpose.

_____
_____
_____
_____
_____
_____
_____
_____
_____
_____
_____
_____
_____
_____
_____
_____
_____
_____
_____
_____
_____
_____

In 2 Corinthians 4:16-18, Paul encourages us not to lose heart, as our inner self is being renewed day by day. Reflect on a time when you felt weary or discouraged in your spiritual journey. How did God renew your strength and remind you of your purpose during that time? Write about the specific ways you experienced His encouragement and guidance, and how it helped you refocus on your calling.

_____
_____
_____
_____
_____
_____
_____
_____
_____
_____
_____
_____
_____
_____
_____
_____
_____
_____

Paul also reminds us in 2 Corinthians 4:16-18 to focus on the eternal rather than the temporary, as our present troubles are preparing us for an eternal glory that far outweighs them all. Consider a challenging situation you are currently facing or have faced in the past. How can you shift your perspective to view this challenge through the lens of eternity and God's ultimate purpose for your life? Write about the ways this change in mindset can help you find peace and hope amidst your present struggles.

_____
_____
_____
_____
_____
_____
_____
_____
_____
_____
_____
_____
_____
_____
_____

DAY 19

See & Believe It

One of my mentors in the faith had a saying that went like this: You got to see it, to see it before you can see it.

It's one of those sayings that makes you scratch your head a little, yet it is a golden gem of faith.

The author of Hebrews says, "Faith is the substance of things hoped for and evidence of things unseen."

Faith is a powerful force that transcends our human understanding, often challenging us to believe in something even before we see it. It is the unwavering trust in God's promises and the conviction that He will fulfill His plans for our lives, despite any obstacles or uncertainties we may face. By embracing faith, we open ourselves to the possibility of experiencing the divine in our everyday lives, allowing us to witness miracles and blessings that might otherwise remain hidden. This steadfast belief in the unseen enables us to navigate life's challenges with courage and hope, knowing that God's love and guidance are always present. As we cultivate our faith, we learn to see the world through the eyes of our Creator, recognizing His hand at work in every aspect of our lives and strengthening our connection to God's purpose for our lives..

Doubt can often creep into our thoughts, making it difficult to trust in our purpose and ourselves. Reflect on a time when doubt threatened to derail your progress towards fulfilling your purpose. How did you rely on your faith to overcome these feelings of uncertainty and continue moving forward? Write about the strategies you used to strengthen your faith and regain confidence in your path.

_____
_____
_____
_____
_____
_____
_____
_____
_____
_____
_____
_____
_____
_____
_____
_____

We have talked for the last few weeks about your purpose and where you want to be. I want you to take a minute and write your future self a letter. Tell yourself how proud you are of what you have accomplished. Speak to your future self about the things you hope to accomplish. See it now so you can see it in the future.

_____

_____

_____

_____

_____

_____

_____

_____

_____

_____

_____

_____

_____

_____

_____

_____

_____

_____

_____

_____

DAY 20

Reflecting on Your Journey

You have been on an incredible journey of self-discovery and finding your purpose. I hope you have learned about yourself and God's plan for your life.

Reflection and self-discovery play a critical role in uncovering and embracing our God-given purpose. By regularly engaging in introspection, we create space to listen for divine guidance and discernment, helping us align our lives with the values and principles of our faith. Through self-discovery, we uncover the unique gifts and talents bestowed upon us by our Creator, which enables us to serve others and fulfill our spiritual calling more effectively. Ultimately, reflection and self-discovery foster a deeper connection with our faith and our purpose, empowering us to live authentically and wholeheartedly in pursuit of our divine mission.

Reflect on what you have learned and what God has spoken to you Write out a list of what you learned and what you will need to get where you and God want.

_____
_____
_____
_____
_____
_____
_____
_____
_____
_____
_____
_____
_____
_____
_____
_____
_____
_____
_____
_____
_____
_____
_____

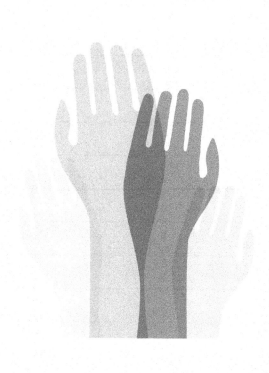

DAY 21

Recommit To Your Purpose

Here we are on Day 21!

So much has changed, mostly you.

We have discussed our purpose, what it looks like, what it will cost, and what God wants to do through you. I am excited for you because I know that God has good things in store for you that only you can do.

I want to spend our last day together as we did on Day 1. As you "press on to lay hold of the reason Jesus laid hold of you," think about what you wrote for your purpose statement.

Has it changed? Do you want to add to it?

Take a few minutes and write down your purpose statement again.

Now write down your vision statement.

What are your core values?

Use these as your compass to guide you as you set out to lay hold of your purpose. Remember that the only thing that matters is that God gets the glory, and His kingdom is advanced here on Earth.

Dear Jesus,

I come to you today with a heart full of gratitude for the journey of discovering my purpose in You. Thank You for the opportunities You have provided me to explore my talents, passions, and gifts and use them to serve others.

Thank You for revealing to us Your unique plan for our lives and guiding us on this path of discovery. We are grateful for the times of joy and fulfillment that we have experienced as we have followed Your leading and for the times of challenge and growth that have helped us to become more like You.

Lord, we recognize that our purpose in You is not just about our own journey but also about the impact we can have on others. Thank You for the people You have placed in our lives who have encouraged, challenged, and supported us along the way.

We pray that You would continue to guide us on this journey of purpose, that we would always seek to honor You in all that we do, and that our lives would reflect Your love and grace to those around us.

In Your precious name, we pray, Amen.

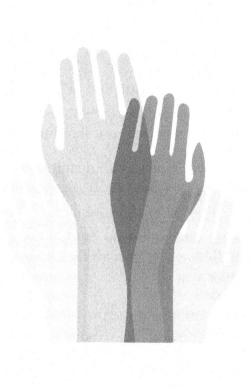

Your Purpose Continues

This is the end of our time together but this is not the end of your process. This is where the real journey begins.

I encourage you to keep journaling and searching for where God wants to use your gifts and talents. Whether starting a new project, volunteering in your community, advocating for a cause, or simply making a small but meaningful gesture toward someone in need, now is the time to act.

Remember, every action counts, and even the smallest act of kindness or effort can make a big difference. So take the initiative and be the change you want to see in the world before someone else makes a change you do not want to see.

Let's commit to taking action, be proactive, and positively impact the world. Together, we can create a better future for ourselves and future generations.

As a Christian, I believe our faith calls us to action in many ways. Here are a few examples:

Love your neighbor as yourself - This is the second greatest commandment according to Jesus (Matthew 22:39). As Christians, we are called to love and care for others, regardless of their race, religion, or social status. This means we should actively seek ways to serve and help those in need. Serve at a food shelf or a homeless shelter.

Share the Gospel - We are also called to share the good news of Jesus Christ with others (Matthew 28:19-20). This means telling people about God's love, grace, and forgiveness and inviting them to become followers of Jesus.

Seek justice and mercy - The Bible is full of passages that call us to seek justice for the oppressed and mercy for the marginalized (Isaiah 1:17, Micah 6:8, James 1:27). This means standing up for those who are being mistreated, advocating for their rights, and showing compassion to those who are suffering. Think of foster children or orphans that need love and the elderly who need a friend.

Care for God's creation - As Christians, we believe that God created the world and everything in it and that we are called to be stewards of his creation (Genesis 1:26-28, Psalm 24:1). This means taking care of the environment, conserving resources, and working to address issues like climate change and pollution.

Be peacemakers - Jesus said, "Blessed are the peacemakers, for they will be called children of God" (Matthew 5:9). As Christians, we are called to work for peace and reconciliation in our communities, nation, and the world. This means promoting dialogue, understanding, and cooperation among people of different backgrounds and beliefs. Praying for our leadership both nationally and locally. Being the change that you want to see in the world.

These are just a few examples of how Christians can and should be active in the world. Ultimately, our call to action is to love God, love our neighbor, and use our gifts and talents to make a positive difference in the world.

Light For Your Purpose Journey

The Bible has a lot to say about God's purpose for our lives. Use the following scriptures for deeper study, guidance, inspiration, and encouragement along your purpose journey.

•

"The Lord had said to Abram, 'Go from your country, your people and your father's household to the land I will show you. I will make you into a great nation, and I will bless you; I will make your name great, and you will be a blessing. I will bless those who bless you, and whoever curses you I will curse; and all peoples on earth will be blessed through you.'" - Genesis 12:1-3

In this passage, God calls Abram (later renamed Abraham) to leave his homeland and promises to bless him and his descendants. This is the beginning of God's plan to create a chosen people through whom He would bring salvation to the world. This verse reminds us that God has a purpose for our lives and that we are part of His greater plan for humanity.

•

"Now if you obey me fully and keep my covenant, then out of all nations you will be my treasured possession. Although the whole earth is mine, you will be for me a kingdom of priests and a holy nation." - Exodus 19:5-6

Here, God speaks to the Israelites through Moses, emphasizing their unique calling as His chosen people. This passage teaches us that obedience to God's commands and living as a holy nation are key aspects of fulfilling His purpose for our lives and the world.

•

"But now, this is what the Lord says— he who created you, Jacob, he who formed you, Israel: 'Do not fear, for I have redeemed you; I have summoned you by name; you are mine. When you pass through the waters, I will be with you; and when you pass through the rivers, they will not sweep over you. When you walk through the fire, you will not be burned; the flames will not set you ablaze.'" - Isaiah 43:1-2

In this passage, God speaks through the prophet Isaiah to comfort Israel during a time of exile. He assures them of His presence and protection, emphasizing that He has called them by name. This verse reminds us that God knows us intimately and has a purpose for our lives.

•

"I will also make you a light for the Gentiles, that my salvation may reach to the ends of the earth." - Isaiah 49:6

This verse is part of the prophecy about the Servant of the Lord (Jesus), who would bring salvation not only to Israel but also to the Gentiles. It highlights God's plan to extend His grace and mercy to all people, emphasizing the importance of sharing the message of salvation with others.

•

"For we are God's handiwork, created in Christ Jesus to do good works, which God prepared in advance for us to do."
 - Ephesians 2:10

✶

In this letter from Paul to the Ephesians, he affirms that we are created by God with a specific purpose – to do good works. This verse encourages us to seek out and fulfill the plans that God has prepared for us in advance.

•

"In their hearts humans plan their course, but the Lord establishes their steps." - Proverbs 16:9

This proverb teaches us that while we may make plans for our lives, it is ultimately God who directs our path. It challenges us to trust in God's guidance and to surrender our own desires and ambitions to His will.

•

"The Lord makes firm the steps of the one who delights in him;" - Psalm 37:23

In this Psalm, David reflects on the faithfulness of God to those who delight in Him. He emphasizes that when we take joy in the Lord, He will guide our steps and establish our path. This verse reminds us of the importance of seeking God's will and delighting in His presence

•

"'For I know the plans I have for you,' declares the Lord, 'plans to prosper you and not to harm you, plans to give you hope and a future.'" - Jeremiah 29:11

Written during Israel's exile, God speaks through the prophet Jeremiah to assure His people that He has a plan and purpose for their lives. This verse encourages us to trust in God's promises and to believe that He has a good and hopeful future for us.

"I press on toward the goal to win the prize for which God has called me heavenward in Christ Jesus." - Philippians 3:14

In his letter to the Philippians, Paul shares his personal commitment to pursuing God's calling on his life. This verse challenges us to remain steadfast in our pursuit of God's will and to press on toward the heavenly goal He has set before us.

•

"But you are a chosen people, a royal priesthood, a holy nation, God's special possession, that you may declare the praises of him who called you out of darkness into his wonderful light."
-1 Peter 2:9

In this letter, Peter addresses the early Christians, reminding them of their unique identity as God's chosen people. This verse emphasizes the importance of living out our calling by declaring God's praises and sharing the good news of Christ with others.

•

"Then Jesus came to them and said, 'All authority in heaven and on earth has been given to me. Therefore go and make disciples of all nations, baptizing them in the name of the Father and of the Son and of the Holy Spirit, and teaching them to obey everything I have commanded you. And surely I am with you always, to the very end of the age.'"- Matthew 28:18-20

In this passage, Jesus commissions His followers to spread the gospel and make disciples of all nations. This Great Commission is a key aspect of God's purpose for our lives, as it helps to fulfill His plan for the world by bringing salvation to all people.

•

"And we know that in all things God works for the good of those who love him, who have been called according to his purpose."
-Romans 8:28

In this verse, Paul assures believers that God is working in their lives for their ultimate good. It reminds us that even when we face trials and difficulties, God is orchestrating events to fulfill His purpose for our lives and the world.

•

"In him we were also chosen, having been predestined according to the plan of him who works out everything in conformity with the purpose of his will, in order that we, who were the first to put our hope in Christ, might be for the praise of his glory."- Ephesians 1:11-12

Paul emphasizes that God has chosen believers according to His plan and purpose. This passage highlights the importance of living our lives in a way that glorifies God and aligns with His will, ultimately contributing to His plan for the world.

•

"Then I saw a new heaven and a new earth, for the first heaven and the first earth had passed away, and there was no longer any sea. I saw the Holy City, the new Jerusalem, coming down out of heaven from God, prepared as a bride beautifully dressed for her husband. And I heard a loud voice from the throne saying, 'Look! God's dwelling place is now among the people, and he will dwell with them. They will be his people, and God himself will be with them and be their God. He will wipe every tear from their eyes. There will be no more death or mourning or crying or pain, for the old order of things has passed away.'" - Revelation 21:1-4

This passage describes the ultimate fulfillment of God's plan for humanity – the creation of a new heaven and a new earth where God dwells with His people. It provides hope and encouragement to Christians, reminding us that our lives are part of God's grand story, which ends in the restoration of all things.

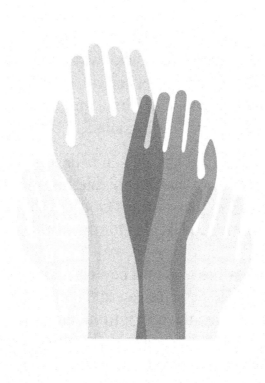

Meet The Author

Gilles Gentley, born in Newport, Vermont, has a heart for redemption and a passion for seeing people grow in their calling. For seventeen years, Gilles has been working in the field of faith-based recovery from addiction, earning him a reputation as a respected voice in that field. He is currently the lead pastor, and occasional bass player, at Catalyst Church in Jericho, Vermont. Gilles is married to his bride, Sarah, and between the two of them, they have six children and one grandchild. Gilles is also a terrible golfer, a lover of the Montreal Canadians, and enjoys fantasy football.

* * * *

If this book has helped you or blessed you I would love to hear from you. If you would like to talk more or do some coaching please feel free to email me at gilles@lifeonpurposecoach.org or visit my website www.lifeonpurposecoach.org.

If you would like to leave me any feedback please reach out to me and let me know. I look forward to hearing from you and if you need prayer please feel free to shoot me a message.

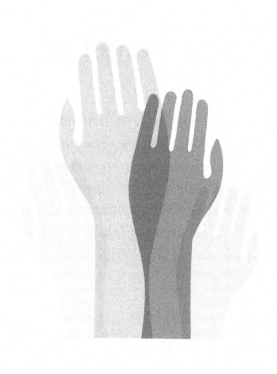

Thank you for choosing Life on Purpose — a part of the Inspirational Journals series.

We hope you've enjoyed the experience.

There are many more journals coming, and we cannot wait to share them with you! To learn more about the Inspirational Journals series and get updates on our new releases, visit:

InspirationalJournalsProject.com

Share Your Feedback

If you could take a minute to review this journal on Amazon, that would be really awesome. :)

Do You Love The Idea of Creating Your Own Inspirational Journal?

Imagine having your own Inspirational Journal. Literally any topic can be leveraged and transformed into a beautiful journal format—and I'm here to help you walk through the process with ease. Inspirational Journals is a program for coaches, consultants, entrepreneurs, business professionals, ministry leaders, and other powerful people who want to use their experience and expertise to guide readers through a process of breakthrough and transformation in a key area of their lives.

Interested? visit

InspirationalJournalsProject.com for more details